Always Erase

First published in 2022 by Blue Diode Press
30 Lochend Road
Leith
Edinburgh EH6 8BS
www.bluediode.co.uk

ISBN: 978-1-915108-00-5

Typesetting: Rob A. Mackenzie.
text in Pilgrim LT Roman

Cover art: © Fee Scroggie, 'Memoria Extraneus'(2016)
Cover design and typography: Rob A. Mackenzie

Diode logo design: Sam and Ian Alexander.

Printed and bound by Imprint Digital, Exeter, UK.
https://digital.imprint.co.uk

For Polly —

Always Erase

Wishing you every inspiration.

~~Lauren Pope~~

L. Pope

Blue Diode Press
Edinburgh

For my sister

So you ate a beetle, big deal!

Contents

I

II

III

I

Fortune, 27th July 2017:
I've wanted out of that cookie for a long time.

Our Lady of the Macabre

What news of the man who keeps his red-bellied macaw
in the freezer, unable to accept its death? Oh please –
like you've never cried in the mirror, nor yet wallowed at this
    altar.
Partake in the sorrow left at the feet of Our Lady:
roses carved out of radishes, the girl who whispers 'blue babies'
in the bath, grandma's Botox addiction – vials of injectable
    filler.
Feel sorry for the basket of poisonous apples
for they know not what they do. Be haunted,
but be handsome too. Above all, be the beautiful sister
wearing velvet frocks at tea time, whose family hangs their
    happiness from her
as from the Yuletide tree. The sister with the best marriage
    prospects,
despite never having so much as posted a letter (you can manage
a household, can't you?). Be the girl in the novel
with consumption – tragic like. Die already. When you rise,
be the sister of whom no one has ever heard.

The times I didn't use my name

When I was the [   ] between two sounds, a thought in their heads,
a penny oxidising at the bottom of the well, the fabric of becoming
        before the simplest

                                                    linguistic act,

before I howled
                ME   and felt the warm wind, the buoyancy of it,

                                        being raised like a flag.

                        *

Picture yourself as a question in the mouths of others.

                                        That's how it was –
the elongated year I learned that staring is the truest expression
                                                    of interest.

            People asked questions –
                    Where do you live?
                            Why aren't you in school? –
            the way a hammock rocks

        against its chain.

            Chloe was a decoy, a name I borrowed –
                            believe me, I was equine –
                            from Fashion Star Fillies.

                        *

Ferns burst arrogantly from impossible places;

on my CV, the words *extrovert* and *people-person*.

My kinship lies with the moonflowers –
a mess of anaemic sisters
bruising under the scrutiny.

*

On the sign-in sheet at Planned Parenthood:

You don't expect to be here when your 40
C'mon Barbie/ Jenny from the Block/ Bonita Applebum
Pulling out method
Young & dumb

My second visit   I wrote VOID, in all caps,

like it was a request.

*

I was thinking about my walls, I was thinking
about the yellow cliffs   eroding
along the coastline;
if I am to be named one thing,
let it be that

& then a woman hollered at me on the road.

We were friends in TZ, many years back.
I didn't respond, kept walking, but it was quite something to be
reminded
of that life
like stepping into old shoes – both mine, and not;
forced into a discarded skin.

13

Vile Jelly

It would have been easy
to go sexy for Halloween
like that woman on *Come Dine With Me*,
who, when hungry, said things like,
'I am so ravished'
(when she meant 'famished').

SEXY: that slinky adjective
followed by an unassuming noun
to describe things that aren't actually appealing at all –
a bunny rabbit, jail bait, an off-the-clock crossing guard –
but become so on Halloween.

You did not want me to be any of these things.
You said,
'what about your dignity, your originality?'
your tipped glass condescending
towards the table
in a reliquary of candlelight.

So, on Halloween night
I am Gloucester's eyeball, and you
are Cornwall's sword.
I am wrapped in a sheet, crouching behind
a circular cardboard cut-out,
you are yourself, in jeans and a t-shirt,
holding a blade made from foil.

Eyeballs speak in movements –
a glance to the side, a twitch, a dilation,
but I am a fake eyeball
so I do not speak at all,

though every time you yell
'Out, vile jelly! Where is thy lustre now?'
and pierce me with your sword,
I hope you know my eyes are rolling.

Proverb

When you say, 'the fig that bleeds milk is not ripe,'
it sounds like a proverb. Through the window

I turn my head to better view the landscape. Gold grass hills
have beached around Vinci, and my mind goes to my hair –

bleached into brittle strands of straw, an obsession with light
perhaps. Still, like a niggle or a sting from a fire ant,

all I can think is that I don't like the way you're holding that fig,
the way it unsettles this moment – and others to come –

so that now, when your hand moves to my lower back,
I think of it as a root grounding me to you, an umbilicus.

My gaze settles on the walled geometry of a courtyard
and the male figure of a Roman statue, armless, inside.

Hinterland

a compilation of autocorrected
and predictive text messages

figure girl video pretty,
through husband grab
lodging, root the cold
from the house.

he wants you twirled
as his morning meeting, a Rubik
of offline fjords; mapped out
little Jigsaw Monster,
blueprint spectre.

but your hobby-fed lips
do not eat the ghost
of chicken hiccups, sip
the amethyst of bedbugs.

figure girl video pretty,
you are always erase.

Miscarriage

I'm told
the moonstone
I carried
in the palm
of my hand
could not alone
will a living thing
to term,

and the eggs eaten
out of superstition
(upside down
on a Sunday)
once held
the same possibility
for which I grieve.

Sometimes things
that do not exist
are real –
the way my ears
hear Etta James
sing 'Cadillac'
not 'At Last,' or how
the opening acoustics
to 'Little Wing'
are, to me, a mimesis
of drowning.

Announce this: today,
the colour of failure
is the robin's
sanguine throat.

Backstage

when my bread belly
wastes
from the habit
of denial
and the dark whip
inside of me
is somehow fed
in the process

when I tourniquet
my words
so that 'unravelled'
ravels again, 'inchoate'
slims to a whole

when I'm so thin
you can no longer
see me
unless the light
fractures
the windows
just so

watch me be as lithe
as airborne dust
that settles
on the necks
of androgynous swans
suspended
from the rafters

Tinder for the Baroque Age

Even in the portrait's darkest corner,
there is still enough light dispersed
to make out the folds of onyx silk
beneath her bosom:
she is wealthy to be sure, this widow.
Her expression, the correct shade
of downcast, brands her desirable.

Three hundred miles away,
where no one knows her yet,
a merchant receives the likeness, peels off
its protective muslin layer; he approves
of the way she honours the deceased,
studies the drapery that accentuates
her still-childbearing hips.

Theatre

And then I was turned inside out, like jeans just out of the wash, a collapsible Silicon cup you take hiking. When they spoke it was not to me but to the concept of me, and to the homunculus. Everything was directed to the homunculus. The men and women elbow-deep inside of me were not alien – I was. Alien even to those who were present and cared, but could not bear to look. Was it really like that? Yes, then no, and then maybe. Do not rely on the person it happened to to tell the story.

How quickly the mind breaks down. No one wanted to touch me; no one wanted to leave me alone. A strange world of masquerade ensued. I lied when I wore makeup. I lied when I showered and styled my hair. I lied to feel a semblance of power: a big fat hook gleaming through my cheek. And now, I have whole friendships that compete in the realm of deceits. I am the act of perpetual hair twirling – not the finger, not the hair: the actual compulsion. Aren't all little girls told to be compulsions when they grow up?

Sometimes I want to walk up to people on the street and say, 'don't you think the Anna Kareninas and Emma Bovarys have suffered enough? How can accommodation and chasteness be housed in one body?' Some day, the homunculus will also need to be asked this. Quietly kiss the cement and weep and think of those who are boundless, and blurred, and gasping. Think of me as the hands shaking your shoulders to wake you up.

Elsewhere

I see doors in eyelets of lace,
          key latches,
               bolt holes.

I stare at the washer's rolling belly,
wonder how it would feel
          to crawl inside,
               be forgotten for a cycle.

I think of Narnia, often,
          the White Witch, and her bounty
              of Turkish delight.

I contemplate the space beyond the light socket,
the black coves of cornicing,
          the perfect o
              of the baby's dark mouth.

I look for the crack in my neighbour's fence
          that leads to a garden,
              that leads to another garden
that leads to a derelict field.

I watch strands of my hair
          worm through the shower drain;
              a drain that ends up where?

I hear muffled voices off the street
          carry through the window,
their thoughts that ramble
          this way, that.

My face reflected on the glass –
          I am a woman; I could be any woman.

Funeral for my Younger Self

I used to be a whole person, with fully formed thoughts.
I used to smoke mushrooms, and think profoundly
as I watched the sun, larger than usual, swallow the Earth
in tender, halcyon light. Now I take my child's medicine
and wait for the pain to become an unformed cloud. It's good,
though, like nostalgia is good, and it does the trick, too.
Oh Asclepius, why does my medicine cabinet always run dry?
In what way does this mother's guilt serve me?
A plague on your reptilian side-eye!

At Starbucks – cracked rib, another swig – the barista's name
is *A. – Asclepius*? I tell him coughing caused my injury
(sympathy, please!). He asks, 'Are you really so fragile?'
Show him the scar dammit, the sunroof your son
entered the world through. Say, *How do you like them stitches*?
Now that the medicine's talking, I point out a cracked rib
signals a beginning, not an end, but he just looks at me
like he looks at all the self-medicated mothers – doe-eyed,
so untouched by life I want to punch him in the face.

Fugue

after Donna Stonecipher

It was like wondering whether to will the thought away, ultimately deciding to just keep smiling through your teeth, hoping that your brain would be a hermit crab – timid to the pursuit of truth.

It was like accepting that the truth is not always the lived truth. It was like milk teeth – the conundrum – whether to care for them or not. Were they real? Did it matter? It was a gift to squander, when a second chance is a certainty.

It was like making a list of all the things you know to be certain: 1) a mother who chooses a favourite is human (and that is not meant kindly); 2) colour is an emergent property of light.

It was like being at a cocktail party and telling everyone that cities are an emergent property of human interaction, as if they didn't know. It was like watching a form of contrived conversation spin wildly out of control. It's hard not to hate your mother in moments like these: *chitchat* like the clearing of her throat.

It was like clearing your throat to speak, and nobody hearing you over the 'wild' conversation – *The offspring of a lion and a tiger is called a liger*! In moments like these, you do not know whether you are invisible or just melting.

It was like wondering whether you are the perpetrator of your own invisibility. Some people are *so* their names, you know? Your name is the gum beneath the desk. Other days, an apostrophe, a radiator on low.

It was like suspecting that the radiator near your restaurant table is on, only to realise that the rioja has turned you into your own internal heat source. Either way, you have missed the conversation. Stains have blossomed in your armpits.

It was like living in one of those armpit towns in a country's middle bit, where every room has a view of the motorway, and where everyone wonders if the motorists can see them naked as they change. Is it worse to be seen or not?

It was like being naked at the spa, on your *relaxing spa day*, in front of your twin, who exercises and cleanses regularly, and who has never had kids. There was a time when you thought the scar on your lower abdomen was a mouth in the dark, grinning like the Cheshire cat:

Beware of women whose sisters are beautiful.

Sleepwalking

As if they were the heads of children,
I pat the boxes of Cream of Wheat and semolina
in our pantry, shush their hyperbolic branding
further into the dark. The cans of tomato soup
need to be unhuddled, their aluminium lids
always threatening to mouth off to each other.
I post one through the laundry chute, roll another
to the yellow-bellied Bogeyman under the couch.

Even in sleep, the gods must be appeased,
which is why I attempt to reclaim my placenta
from the white mulberry by crooning to it
out the kitchen window: 'This land is your land,
and this land is my land...' but the static tongue
of diving board just looks at me.
Even the pool, and I thought we were friends,
warns me with its absence of water.
I summon Coco Chanel, through the medium of perfume:
What would you do if landed with an obstreperous house?
She tells me she would sprawl out on that diving board
like her body is a feast, like she owns the place,
the whole *putain de maison* – which I do.

II

In the toilet, tissue clings
      to the ceiling:
in the ladies, we call them *paper flowers*;
in the gent's, *spit wads* or *doofers*.
Such imprecise signage on the doors
to describe these half children,
each with their own
      undeveloped star.

Little Sister

She moves around the room
in search of something,
like a hawk kiting on moderate wind
though not as graceful.

"Is the dying thing sad?"
        "Yes, generally the dying thing is sad."

Mimic my cry. Watch how I shake hands,
listen for the crack in my smile –
it will be a faint noise, like the click of a lock
or the earth opening up.

Christina Maria is a shadow
at her granddaddy's funeral in Pocatello.
She repeats what her mother
shouted as they parked the car
and took out the casserole:

*"mommy said we parked
       at the ass-end of space."*

The guests laugh, some sound like cotton balls,
others are nervous like the dirt waiting
to be discovered under the refrigerator.

She thinks she has made a joke, and repeats,
"ass-end of space."

Then the room becomes quiet,
except for the drier's foetal kick
in the room adjoining the kitchen,
and a whisper –

"someday will I die?"
  "Yes, someday you will."
"That will be sad."

Nocturne

She waters the cyclamen –
her hand like a stork's beak
delivers packages of ice
from her vodka tonic.

At the vanity, she plucks
long static teardrops
from her ears,
places them in the jewellery box
the way a child,
or the memory of one,
is put to bed.

Pen Pals

Why wasn't I the kind of girl who drew smiles and frowns,
winks and upside down
faces in the dots of her i's,
like Becci, who pencilled in hearts and stars,
and left a lipstick kiss at the foot of the page
abutting "Yours,"?
You always knew how Becci felt, gushing
like a knocked over hydrant.

I once wrote Becci a letter with words like *bikini,*
militia and *rhinitis* in the same run-on sentence,
imagining the dots of my i's floating
towards the surface/ margin.
Would she burden them, on my behalf,
with emotion?
As if my letters were houseplants
etiolating in the absence of light,
Becci often asked,
> *How are you, really?*

> I felt
I owed her something –
calligraphy on lavender-scented paper,
prettily packaged snippets
of keratin.

I always imagined including a postscript like
sometimes I picture the faces you've drawn in the dots of
  your i's
among Charlie's and his granddad's at the Wonka Factory
before the whirring of the giant overhead fan...

press / preserve

There were better ways to admire the half-eaten
cherry leaves

than to press them between the pages
of a dictionary.

We tied each stem with fishing line,

hung them

at staggered heights against the window.

The youngest of us called it sheet music;

we understood

in the way we understand a shape with soft edges

in the distance.

We watched afternoon filter through,

the gaping mouthfuls created a strange arrhythmia

of light.

As the season passed,   the leaves bleached,

                              curled in on themselves.

The eldest of us called it a row of hatched chrysalides;

                                        we understood

in the way we understand that a circle has no end.

The days thinned in winter, the leaves had some respite.

Those of us without a superlative to amplify ourselves

said that the leaves were just leaves;

this was understood

in the way we understand the enclosure of a name.

At the Aphasiac's Tea Party

I cannot be sure, though I suspect,
that when you raise your nostrils to the wind
you whiff the ghosts of Apache apricots,
O'Henrys from our orchard – the names of which
you can no more grasp than you can my own.

We sit on a no-name bench, near the no-name lake,
beneath a no-name tree, threading words
for new kennings – butt hug, trout bath, the billowing eye –
while the day progresses into a faraway look
that needs no designation.

Elegy of the Sandcastle

after Anna Journey

If hearing is the last faculty to go,
I need to believe your last moments weren't besieged

by the lady down the hall with the plastic doll pleading,
     'please don't take my baby!'
or the Catholic nurse muttering, 'Miss Evelyn, go to the
     light you wretch'

because you mocked her foreign accent with your
     Southern drawl
that stretched vowels into long afternoons on your daddy's
     porch in the Ozarks

where you learned as a girl how to make insults skip
from your lips with the air of a compliment – something I
     could never do.

In your last moments, I need to believe you heard the gulls
     overhead
and the sound of the ocean rocking the shore with a swell;

our voices buoyant as we held you in our hands
weaving you with the sand between our fingers,

the wet mixture dripping into turrets and caverns of mud
     and kelp;
the ping of the colander blockading the castle until
     completion.

I need to know the last sound you heard was the crash of surf
splashing over our toes, our ankles and shins –

that final burst of winter that carried you away,
retreating from us like the sound of rolling pebbles.

My Father Tells Me to Get Married

Face paint made
from cephalopod ink,
carob nibs swapped in
for chocolate
buried in a dollop
of dough, Velcro
laces for teens:
you taught us
the outer reaches
of convention.

Whole days went by
without walls defining
our space, except
the dogwood's boughs
draped in a corridor
around our car,
the windows
down.

Scraped elbows,
busted lips
healed by the science
of crystals: Rose Quartz
to soothe; Galena
for inflammation.

Ears to the dirt,
we listened
for a magnetic shift,
the reverse
of the earth clockwise,
knowing we'd never
hear it coming –

like now,
when from nowhere
you assert my unborn child
cares about wedlock.
You're clasping my finger,
and I stare at you
with a mouthful
of flies.

Goodbye, House

When I come, claiming
to be your daughter, please remember
the saltwater that passed between us.

I turn up in the garden,
necking a bottle of Two-Buck Chuck
and clutching a wand of agapanthus
sprung from my departed guinea pig;
I tuck a piece of you beneath my armpit, here,
in the region of tender.

This second union is all over
you – new frock, exotic smell –
in high def. Your new daughter's
glorious laugh jaundices my own.
Oh, be sure to show her how
to practice kissing in the mirror,
her saliva smeared with that very shade
of *StrutYourSlut* I wore.

Petit Socco

Kebab shop, bric-a-brac stalls: she loops
between lapis-hued clothing lines, through
courtyards with fountains, trespasses riads
hunting out carved initials – any sign she lived here
during the comatose years when Westerners
crossed the Strait to smoke and fuck.

The rooms of has-been smoke dens now fucked
by a different type of tourism: ceiling fans loop
overhead so that wealthy westerners
feel comfortable as they voyeur through
the time warp looking glass. No hash here
(unless you want it)! Free love emaciates in the riad's

refurb. Gone is the stained glass, the myriad
of *zellige* tiles, hookah pipes, the master fucking
his harem of wives – the ghostly atmosphere…
I cling to her fringe-trimmed coat, loop-de-looping
through one Moorish door and out through
another as she tells me: 'We aren't that kind of Westerner.'

Even as she says it, I know I'm the hollowest
shade of her bohemian ideal. She inspects the riad's
floorboards for strawberry blonde strands sloughed
from the ghost of her gorgeous mane – 'the most fuckable
thing about her.' She recalls dinners of *loup
de mer*, mint tea, clementine wedges that adhered

to her hunger as we skip from this roof to that, hear
the song of a faith that is anything but Western.
How many milky-eyed moons have looped
the earth since her return to the riad
where the Dutchman asked her to fuck
to the call to prayer? She claims she was throughly

gobsmacked, though something happened through
this maze of intricately carved doors and incoherent
streets to propel us on this kaleidoscopic headfuck –
ugh, family! Like any self-conscious westerner,
I try to blend in, embrace the muddle of ochre riads,
haggle (poorly) for the hand of Fatima now looped

through my strap. At night, we move west
past ethereal storks, nesting along the riads.
The clap clap clap of people fucking on loop.

III

I will myself
to be the sunlight,
a mustard field,
a vase
of Sorrento lemons...

Hijo de puta

The three of us lie side by side; the little one,
a Nosferatu, cabbage-eared and swaddled.

We speak in mime:
I shush you with a well-timed finger
trawled across my throat,
a look as grim as any pioneer's
who crossed The Rockies in winter
and may have eaten a loved one
who perished in the cold;
you retaliate, flip the bird at me,
screwing the air with your finger
like it's some invisible asshole.

All the while the smell of my milk,
sweet on the *putto*'s breath.

Pavement Vomit

A spilled gut spoils
in the light of day. Now
an abstraction of space –
all that food
held together in a fist of yarn
when the night began.

I hope you made it home, Anonymous.
Your stomach's contents –
now a cairn to last night's exploits –
seem too personal
for my morning commute.
I try not to look, but do.

Photoshop

Girl with the shaved crotch:
breathy and fuchsia-cheeked,
hot-house head of flowers and fruits
nestled into a plaited crown
the colour of a Bavarian pretzel.

Why, now that she has my face,
can you not recognise me as the Olympia
of the produce aisle?
Is it that I've spent a lifetime
rethinking my midriff in your name
or wondering whether my tits speak
the language of perfect clip?
If my behaviour's *au courant*?

I've been sliced bread
          in the name of perfection, a closed door,
a severed stem; in the name of perfection
I allowed silence, mistook it
for perfection; I've become the doll
          inside the doll inside for you.

There are times I want to claw
my image on your bicep, there,
where we can both see it –
in ink as black as rage
cloaked in calm.
          Where we can really see it.

More Asleep Than Dead

Before long
you will spend more time
in the garden with the barbecue
burning the drying brush –
a christening of grey-blue ash –
until you're ankle deep in it.

And I will be inside
retreating further into rooms
you don't enter anymore,
and for some time we will pretend
like two people orbiting
the same sinuous truth –
that ribbon of diaphanous silk –
like the people of Pompeii who,
overcome by shock,
still believed the crops
were just burning.

Through anything other than scissored fingers

a chorus of angels in perfect hierarchy –
church is funny like that – tiers of seraphim, cherubim
& thrones. Imagine needing a throne to access god, like
needing a dining chair to reach the top-shelf porcelain.
O father, son, holy domesticity! Church is a good place
for thinking – your inner face can be a black-eyed flower
whilst everyone is lost in their thoughts & not observing.
For instance, you can ponder your nature, the equivalency
of looking through scissored fingers. Please don't say
peeping through keyholes. One means 'reluctant to know,'
& the other 'eager for information.' Imagine a world
where your skin is a fresco on the ceiling
of the Sistine Chapel. You hold many secrets; you know
so little of the actual world – sun-kissed, salt-bleached,
begging to be touched.

/Meditation on Childhood/

Her speech wheels;
I know the wine has loosened the usual bolts
that keep her upright.

We slip into memory – those after school afternoons
when a kid gets so bored she goes in search of something,
like the chrysalises latched to the back of marble headstones
lining the garden wall.

Her voice tapers –
                 a trail of breadcrumbs.
I tread lightly, listen,
count tadpoles crossing the vitreous humour,
close my eyes to the sun,
discover the smell of oatmeal and SPF.

She tells me she once crawled inside the boat
in the garage – the whole hull shimmered
with mother-of-pearl scales.
         She lay on her back
listening to footsteps – mine and Danny's –
                          fumbling overhead.

With the fishing poles, she uncovered
a Remington so old it looked to her like treasure.
She became buccaneer – her ship, the *Hispaniola*,
sailed the Tortuga sea. Voice weathered by rum,
she croaked like a seabird, 'Fight or die by this gun!'

When she says the barrel fitted perfectly
         to the temple of her head,
I feel its coolness inch through me.
My life becomes a sun-scorched lawn.

I'm afraid to move, afraid to speak, afraid my breath,
                    like the flap of a wing,
will affect the outcome of that moment.

She sinks into the lounge chair –
we're poolside, sipping Viognier

            so I think she must be real.

Addenda to my Sister's Personality

a. if the meaning of the condition wasn't known, she
might describe the word pleurisy as birdcall, based on
its sound.

b. fact: trees are emotional anaemics. They reach and
reach and reach and reach.

c. 'If I could name myself, I'd choose *velour blanket*.'

d. when taking a photograph of a group of strangers,
always be a perfectionist, even though it is unlikely
you will ever see them again.

e. there is logic beyond the folds of time and linen.

f. if presented with the opportunity, she would wrap
herself in a capillary, stroke its hair-like thinness.

g. check for hitch-hiking bedbugs. After guests visit,
inspect beds, carpets, upholstered furniture. Assume
it's bad, especially if they are your kin.

h. 'Forest Lawn is an oxymoron; do not, whatever you do,
bury me there.'

i. make-up brushes should sweep in a downwards motion.
Always, always.

Hold

I

I make breathing a profession
as I wait for your hands.

Your hands rummaging like that, your hands in the backseat –
feeling for loose change, I think.

Your hands like the sugar-coated shell of a candied almond,
wrist deep in wet plaster; what I could lick from those hands…

if you'd let me. I have ways of keeping time.

When Marvin Gaye played, I knew not to open the door
to my parents' bedroom for 3 minutes and 58 seconds plus one
    repeat.

I tell you this
as your hand thrums the engine of a '66 mustang convertible
the colour of a silver lining.

You hide in that cloud; I undress in this way.

The distance from your hands to your shoulders
raised earwards
is equal in length to the meaningful stare you are so intent

on denying me.
I have ways of keeping time.

II

I went to school with April Gaye, Marvin's niece. No one said
    to her,
your grandfather's a murderer, but they were thinking it.
April was quiet, like you are quiet, which I mistook for sweet.

You are quiet / contemplative, but your hands are shouty
when they grab my waist and lift me to x.

Time stops.

My sister says *shouty* is the wrong adjective. I know what it is
    like to hit a wall
at high speed, or to be stranded –
not like on an island, but like a wheel on the side of the road in
    a desert.

The right adjective scares me.

My sister says I am the neck on that chicken you broke at army
    camp.

When I breathe down the phone, and it sounds like *Just one,
    baby,*
my sister says I'm an addict.

                Hello?
Maybe you are not contemplative. Maybe I misjudged you.

III

Who could I tell
that I wanted to be the sweat on the bodies grinding
in that smoky room in the opening scene of *Dirty Dancing*?
Beads of neck-loving curvature, salt poesy.

Who could I tell that I would one day be alone and crying in a
    room the size of a fist,
cut like the pierced flesh between my legs?

After the riots, we flocked to the suburbs –
white flight was a frozen lake around our ankles.
I have ways of keeping time. Exact time.
Marriage loops when there is nothing to say or do.
Marvin Gaye was in elevators.
Marvin Gaye was at the Department of Motor Vehicles.
Marvin Gaye was in the feminine hygiene aisle at the grocery.
Marvin Gaye was buried, again and again, like Bob Marley is
    buried under every college
dorm room of the last three decades. Bundling time like this is
    conventional –
something I picked up in suburbia.

IV

On hold waiting for a call centre representative:

Ain't that peculiar.
A peculiar-arity.
Ain't that peculiar, baby?
Peculiar as can be.

V

You're going for a lamb dhansak with the guys from church.
What church? Did we / Do we/ Have we *ever* gone to church?

Marvin Gay Sr. was a Pentecostal minister.

I tell my sister I can make a curry; she says this is not about
  me. I hang up
on her a lot: hang up, hang up, hang-up. I have ways of
  keeping time.

/Prenatal Meditation/

The question: *How much weight have you gained?*
        will repeat itself
                until I am again a sliver of branch.

I canter beyond the row of elms, a branch lashes my cheek
        as I go, torso no longer bending forward
                the way it used to.

I gallop until the question cracks beneath the weight
        of hooves: gain ground, speed, distance.
                I become singular and whole

like a bullet exiting the shoulder blade, whistling
        with the rage of all women made to feel
                less than holy.

Like when I spread my legs for comfort in front of the TV,
        and your sulky hand finds a second home
                between my thighs.

Am I the kind of thirst that haunts you
        when you flick on the lights at 2am
                for a stale glass of water

only to return to bed to find me larger,
        and more threatening
                than I was nine months ago?

Call me dumpling, turnip, a fat round pie
        as you sink further into me
                than either thought was possible.

Mauna Loa

Fissures warp the surface,
sulphur surrounds the roots
of silversword and palm.
We hear the pop
of foliage stunned by lava.
We make lists as we walk
of the things I am not supposed to do
(like this), register
the temperature of the earth
against each footstep, wind our way
to where the molten lava
meets the ocean. I will tell him
he witnessed it inside of me
tangentially, remembering
how my mother said the same.
Pele's Hair streams downwind
in the distance, a reminder
to walk the way we came.

REPETITION [rɛprɪ'tɪʃ(ə)n]

1 : half nap, eyes closed to the flat screen realm /of televised tennis. Every shriek is mirrored /on the opposite side of the court. /In this way, I can see the ball /move back and forth.

2 : Klein Blue /is the colour of my true love's hair... /my love is like a monochrome rose. Dear /Yves, eves, ease: / your name is a water park wave /rolled from my lips.

3 : I said to the cave, 'Hello there.' My words left, /became something /else. /A second later, the cave sang /back. It said it to the point of meaninglessness, /and then we sat in silence.

/KonMari Meditation/

I am a lotus. I count to 10 to keep my mind in check. Picture a flickering light; focus on it. Do I need to be a temple? I could just be a house. A temple is visited on occasion; I housed another being while he grew. I watched his things – his pillow, his bedding, his small comforts – ooze out of me like a long, wet, slippery song. If my face looks serene, will my mind follow? The answer is a nest of Russian dolls – keep looking.

We celebrate the downsizing from one house into another. So much of our time spent in-house, house-bound, feeling house-proud. Beneath all this flesh is the chiselled potential, squinting sideways into the vacant space of a gallery wall. I am a lotus. Imagine a flame. Imagine an empty room. If I were to build my selves into perfect right-angled squares, they would be too beautiful.

Notes

Miscarriage: "Little Wing" is a song by Jimi Hendrix.

Elsewhere: was commissioned for the SEEN / UNSEEN project: a collection of ekphrastic responses to the 'Hidden Gems' exhibition at the City Arts Centre in Edinburgh. The poem was written in response to Anthony Hatwell's 'Face of a Woman.'

Fugue: the last line is taken from Valentine Penrose's surrealist poem collage, *Dons des Féminines* (1951).

Hijo de Puta: translates broadly from Spanish as 'son of a bitch.'

More Asleep Than Dead: the title comes from Pliny the Younger's description of his uncle's body after the eruption of Vesuvius at Pompeii (*Epistulae VI*).

Hold: 'I have my ways of keeping time' is a line taken from Jane Yeh's "Correspondence," published in her first collection, *Marabou*.

Mauna Loa: Pele is the Hawaiian goddess of volcanoes. 'Pele's Hair' are fine threads of volcanic glass, formed when a spray of lava cools rapidly in the air.

Acknowledgements

Grateful acknowledgment is made to the editors of the following publications, where these poems, or some version of them, first appeared: *Best New British and Irish Poets 2017, Brotherton Poetry Prize Anthology* (Carcanet), *Gutter, Magma, New Writing Scotland, The North, Poetry Wales* and *The Rialto*.

Recognition to the following organisations and institutions for their generous support: the University of Southern California (David St. John, in particular); the Scottish Universities' International Summer School (SUISS); the Orkney Writers' Course.

Heartfelt thanks and admiration are owed to my teachers, colleagues, and friends at the University of Edinburgh for their encouragement and community: Jonathan Bay, Tim Craven, Alan Gillis, Katy Hastie, Russell Jones, Dorothy Lawrenson, Marianne MacRae, Jane McKie, Alycia Pirmohamed, Sarah Stewart and Calum Rodger. Utmost appreciation to Miriam Gamble for six wonderful years of mentorship, friendship and PhD supervision.

To Rob Mackenzie: I am so thrilled that *Always Erase* has found its home with Blue Diode, thank you.

Warmth and gratitude to my family and friends in California, Scotland and beyond. Most of all, to my beautiful distractions, Ross, Garner and Felix – love you.

Lauren Pope was raised in Los Angeles and lives in Edinburgh. She runs courses in Creative Writing, British Literature and Contemporary British Theatre and Performance at the Scottish Universities' International Summer School (SUISS). Her poetry pamphlet, *Announce This* (Templar Poetry), was shortlisted for the 2018 Callum Macdonald Memorial Awards. She is a 2019 Manchester Poetry Prize finalist, and winner of the 2021 Brotherton Poetry Prize.